Married to Fatherhood
Volume 1

MARTIN STEWARD

Connect with me:

Facebook.com/mstewardpro1

Twitter.com/mstewardpro

Instagram.com/mstewardpro

LinkedIn.com/in/mstewardpro

Published on Amazon by:

createspace.com

Book cover design by:

mstewardpro.com

© Copyright, All rights reserved, MSteward Pro, LLC.

ACKNOWLEDMENTS TO MY CLOUD

Since we are surrounded by such a great cloud of witnesses, let us throw off everything that hinders and the sin that so easily entangles. *"Hebrews 12:1"*

I have created my own cloud of witnesses, meaning the people that have paved the way for me as my example to the faithfulness of God and assurance that everything will work out for my good. Those that continue to inspire me toward greatness.

-**Eboné Steward**-
-Fred C. Steward-
-Georgella Steward-
-The Late Frederick A. Steward-
-**Pastor Jevah L. Richardson**-
-Bishop Eric K. Clark-
-Bishop TD Jakes-
-Joe McRae-
-Steve Harvey-
-TET Better Life Ministry-

CONTENTS

	Acknowledgments	I
	Dedication	6
1	My Father, My Hero	11
2	I. AM. DAD.	40
3	Discipline	73
4	Provider	111
5	Help Fit	125
6	The Vow	161
	About The Author	173

DEDICATED TO DADDY'S BIG BOY
&
DADDY'S BABY

Jaxon Martin Steward & Violette Ebonae Steward

There has to be a better way to raise kids for me as a father. I have a philosophy that I believe will work. But who has a guarantee that you will not struggle during your development as a father. The beginning stages of anything are both terrifying and very exciting. But over time the exciting things become normal things and lose its wow factor. I always placed this scenario with cars, electronics, jewelry, but never with children. So it stands that even with children you can lose the feeling of excitement you felt when having your child in your arms for the first time. There has to be something that can help you maintain your consistency once normalcy sets in.

This book describes me 2:00 am in the morning trying to let my recovering wife sleep while I manage the kids. When my heart and mind was confused on whether or not I really know what I'm doing. Everything I was doing did not seem to work when putting one to sleep or stop them from crying, the second child woke the first child back up. Those were some rough days. There has to be a better way for me. I am not talking about tips and tricks on a daily basis to help me with parenting but I needed something that could consistently keep my mind at a state of rest that I might gain wisdom to see a better way. If I lose my mind - then I will lose my kids and then ultimately I will lose my family. But if I keep my mind then I maintain my place as the man in my home. It is vitally important that I maintain my place as THE MAN in my home. This process did not even come as a difficulty; it was actually a quite simple transition to understand but a journey to learn.

- Bend the tree while it is tender-

In order for me to explain this, I must take you through some of my mental wilderness experiences that I crawled out of.

MY FATHER, MY HERO

My father is Frederick Augustus Steward. Who I remember him to be, was one that spent a lot of time working. He worked at Independent Beauty Supply in Jersey City, NJ on Monticello Ave. If you want to talk about someone dedicated, my dad worked his job to the core. A few times I actually went to his job, he would take me around showing me what he did and he would call me as we walked through, saying "Marty"! Always making me laugh. It was just the way he said it that I could pick up his voice among millions. Everybody loved my dad, if you want to talk about somebody that was well known my father could walk up and down any block in Jersey City and they would know him.

I didn't know how they all knew him I just knew that he was well known and loved.

My father loved his job, he did inventory for Independent Beauty Supply in Jersey City and he was good at it. You must understand this, that I grew up in an era where you didn't question your parents and one of the questions that I never asked was how much money do you make or are you managing your bills correctly. I just knew that my mom and dad did what they can to take care of us and of course I was included in that number.

My father was a dedicated husband to my mother; one of the things that I can remember is when my mom was arguing with someone in our house and it must have gotten real heated because she threatened to walk out on the whole family. I was sitting in the living room downstairs watching her come down the stairs with bags in hand and she was yelling being very upset then at the same time my dad came flying down the stairs getting in front of her, telling her "You're not going anywhere". My mom meanwhile was yelling at my dad telling him to get off of her but my dad made her go back upstairs as to say, we are in this together and I am not letting you walk away from this family. For me, that was an extreme husband moment that you don't allow your wife to give up, to back down or to let go.

My mom had to deal with some serious struggles back then, putting up with a lot of foolishness and this night she was fed up and getting ready to leave the house! My dad didn't let her though.

What a heavy moment for me.

Growing up, there were a few things my dad and I were able to do, one of which was going to a Yankees baseball game. I'm not a baseball fan or a football fan but by default I am a New York Yankees supporter and a New York Giants supporter because these were my dad's favorite teams, hands down this was my inheritance, my dad loved everything New York. The one time that I can remember us going to a baseball game my younger brother and I were having a great time and during the game, as in any game, there was a fly ball coming so my dad without a glove was able to get the perfect timing and catch this fly ball bare handed. I didn't even question if he was hurt I just looked at him, like how did you just do that? This was my dad, my superhero! These are the things that kept me motivated, that I had my mom and my dad in my life as I grew up.

At the age of thirteen I started going to church, I accepted Jesus into my life and started on a journey that changed my life forever. Mind you this was my decision with accepting the Lord because my parents were not heavily into church; well not as I remember it. I remember my mom taking us on the holidays to church but that was it, I do not remember any level of consistency. My dad didn't go to church as far as I can remember it was my siblings and I who went, something that we chose to do.

I spent a lot of time in church, I

wasn't out in the street acting up as they say drinking, smoking, or having sex. I spent that much time in church and it kept me away from these elements of life. My dad didn't have that active role as far as church is concerned. I can always remember whenever I brought it up he would say, "Marty, Marty come on I don't do that". He always believed that if you're good enough and treat people good that you will make it to heaven and he actually lived his life that way. My dad treated people right never started trouble or made issues with people, he didn't break the law. His life was about his family, bringing money in the house and playing the numbers, he loved playing his numbers. It was a part of his life. This is who he was, which was not centered on church. Strangely, the more that I became dedicated to the church, the more I became distant to my dad; however my mom started coming to the church as a result to our commitment. She saw how deep the commitment to God was and she ended up joining the church but my dad still didn't come. Going to church was not a part of his journey at that time but he respected what I believed. How do I know that he respected my commitment to Christ and the church, because he would make sure that we prayed over our food and from someone who was not centered on church or studied religions, for him to make this acknowledgement had a major meaning. Even when I began to teach and preach in the church he bought me hanker chiefs and I asked him why, his response was that when I preach it's for wiping your mouth. This might have been a small thing for many but for me; it meant the world. It wasn't his desire at the time to commit to Christ the way I did but he had the utmost respect for my commitment to God. However, that's where it stayed. As I spent the bulk of my life being committed to the church there were other things I did outside of church functions, I am an artist, a graphic designer, a playwright, a swimmer, a barber, an actor, a singer, a basketball player, a bowler, a skater, etc. Nonetheless, I still spent majority of my youth in the church and at one point I was there seven days a week.

Sunday was obviously church service but not just any service, it was the stereotypical "Black Church" service where I went in at 10am and stayed until

4pm, sometimes 5pm if the spirit was moving. I don't regret it at all because this is what kept me in those days. Monday was 6pm prayer, Tuesday there was hospital ministry, Wednesday was bible study, Thursday was nursing home ministry, and Friday was deliverance service and all night prayer, which was every Friday night until Saturday morning. Then once a month we had a "shut in" which was Friday night until Sunday morning, but let's not forget about Saturday where we had street ministry. This is when we put the bull horn on top of the car attached to the PA system inside the car and picked three to four locations throughout the city to preach on the street and hand out gospel literature that promotes life telling everyone that Jesus loves and He saves,

He died for our sins, and to hear hope. After being committed for a while I even became a regular on the microphone speaking to the youth out in the open air. This is what kept my mind straight and it kept me from falling into temptation. Keeping this commitment for many years, after a while though I started to struggle because I began to feel that this was all I did with my life like I was missing something.

As I fore stated, I have many talents that were not being utilized or perfected because I spent so much time in the church. Now I was not missing anything in regards to my youth with the desire to be young and foolish.

There were just opportunities that I didn't push myself into because it was a greater need to keep my 7 day a week commitment to the church.

I must clarify that my reasons for not exploring the liberties I could have experienced, such as; The High School Basketball Team where I only tried out once, College Basketball team I only tried out once, Art Clubs, or living on campus during my college years. All these were past over because I never wanted to lose my connection with God as I thought I would. This was not something that was taught in the church that I attended though. This must be made clear because such a philosophy must be considered borderline false doctrine or even a cult but to my benefit this was not taught to me this was rather how I thought I should hold on to Jesus by not letting anything get in my way of what I was doing for God "in the church". At a certain time during this commitment I couldn't shake this feeling of being void, so what I began to do in response to this feeling was I started playing a lot of street ball.

    Street basketball became my crutch, it became my outlet to where I started playing more basketball then I did going to church and in those years trying to fill this void I began to consider the things that I have been missing. So why do you ask did I bring out my great commitment to church and now this struggle to fill this huge void? Why did I start inspecting my life and researching what was missing out of my life?

Because I started to feel like I was missing something from my father. I came to the place of what I call "The Adam Syndrome", this is when you are questioned for what you are doing wrong and you immediately start pointing the finger to someone else instead of owning up to your failure. I tried to find external reasons for my struggle with my internal demons and my conclusion for the source of my problems was, I pointed my finger toward my father. This became very interesting because nobody would think that "I" would put any blame on my dad, but I did.

I remember this exact moment, during my college years I was home sitting on my bed trying to do homework very frustrated because I could not understand it.

I was having a very difficult time understanding my work during my sophomore and junior years of college. Every semester I struggled, I wasn't able to get my books every year until midterms due to financial struggles and every year I fell behind in my classes having to play catch up, I just couldn't get the work. Books or no books I just had difficulty with understanding the work, this was custom even in High School but now on a college level I couldn't take it any more. Sitting on the bed that day I was sick of the struggle being behind the eight ball, why do I have to be in this struggle every year? I began to question is there something wrong with me, is there an actual medical problem with me or is it just something that is missing out of my life.

Now here I am thinking about the very person I felt honored to be my dad, I am directing all of the reasons for my struggles toward. I began to look at an opposing approach toward my dad that when there was an issue in school and someone had to come in and see about me, it was my mom. For parent teacher night my mom came, one incident in High School after showing up late to often I had to serve a Saturday detention and it was my mother who turned the school upside down but never my Dad. My father never came to school to do any of this; he made it to all my graduations but what about the parenting aspect of being a dad. Even growing up from a little child I was never reprimanded by my dad, I never was disciplined by my dad, not like I wanted too but it is something that provides some guidance and it never came from him. My mom was doing all of this work so I began to look at this very intensely. I mean, I remember him every Christmas morning when we opened up presents he monitored all the kids as we opened the gifts, I remember when he took me to the Yankees game and other good memories but where was he in the parenting moments. I remember I would be acting up in our bedroom as a child and not paying attention to the warning of quieting down because it's a school night and again it was my mother who had to come up the stairs and set us straight but my dad was right in the next room and didn't do anything. Why, Why, Why? Where was he in my life to guide me as a man, maybe if he was doing more I wouldn't be struggling like this, just maybe if he provided more parenting I wouldn't be behind the eight ball every semester? I began to have heavy anguish against him and to make it worse, I remembered the time I was headed out to church and walking down the block was my dad stumbling because he had drank too much. Now my parents were no alcoholics but they did drink their beer, my dad drank Budweiser and my mom miller light, I guess fewer calories I don't know. Nonetheless, here he was stumbling and I can remember thinking that this was the first time I actually felt ashamed that I am committed to going to church, trying to live holy and this was my dad I was helping in the house. I would never disrespect my dad, I loved and honored him and we always interacted with conversation and shared laughs but I am trying to put these pieces together in my life of why he never connected with me the way I felt he should have as a father. Maybe this was the reason for my void and I continued to point the finger that maybe he is the reason for my inner issues. Maybe if I didn't lack in these areas I would have been better off in life, that I would have made better decisions which would have caused me to excel and advance. Trying to make sense of all of this, I go talk to my mother because I was not in a good headspace with my father and I got up from where I was, full of all these emotions telling my mom that I am ready to drop out. I could get a job to bring in some extra money, where I know she needed the help so it sounded like a good plan. I told her I was tired of struggling and needed a change after some years I'll go back and do a trade or something but I just didn't like the headspace I was in. So I asked my mom, to better my understanding, can you tell me what is wrong with me? Is there something wrong with me? I didn't say what I felt about my father yet I just wanted to hear her perspective on me. My mom looked at me with a sense of bewilderment and opened up a conversation about me that I have never heard or never thought I would hear as pertains to my life and even my father. After this moment my life would never be the same.

So here I am sitting on my mother's bed preparing myself to hear what she's about say and I kept myself open to whatever. Now that I am in this position and prepared to get some type of help with the way I was feeling, my mother was about to answer me. She first stated that even from a little child my frustration was always there as relates to school. I always had a problem with forgetting and when thinking about it I always had a problem with depression as well. I had a problem loving myself because of the depression. I ask my mom plainly, "Is there something wrong with me"? Did I miss something in my development that is hindering me from reaching my greatest potential? Because I feel like I do not function the way I believe a consistent level of normalcy should function.

So my mom says that during my birth my head pushed against her pelvis bone in a diagonal position, the doctors had to reposition my body from being breach and the umbilical cord wrapped around my neck.

During this process my heart stopped and I died. The doctors managed to revive me by restarting my heart but told my mother that due to these challenges at my birth that it damaged part of my brain and I would be slow for the rest of my life. Then my mother quickly came to my mental rescue after hearing such news sitting on her bed and she told me her response to the doctors was that she really didn't care about their diagnosis just give me my son and let me go home, he will be just fine.

This now brought so much light to my difficulties growing up, the difficulties that I've had with depression because of my challenges with remembering things, or keeping a consistent thought pattern that would help me function even as the stereotypical normal human being. My forgetfulness would cause me to daydream very often, not allowing me to stay focused when I should have in school or home. After we dealt with that issue now I had to deal with the bigger issue and main reason for coming to talk to her, the issues with my dad.

I had to explain to her my need for a father, how I put blame on my father for not being there the way he should have. How she had to come from the bottom floor to the attic to correct our behavior when he was right in the next room.

Times when my siblings and I needed assistance in school she always came and never him, he never came to check up on me.

Why doesn't he have that place in my life? Then my mother looks with a puzzled stare and burst out with laughter. Now I'm confused, seeing I am being so serious and right in the middle of our conversation she starts laughing. What am I missing? She continues and says, in regard to the misbehaving upstairs and she had to come up to deal with us, or the times where parents were needed in the school and she only came to handle the matter. The reason why she spent most of the time talking with us in all these matters and not my dad is because he could not hear us acting up or hear people in open rooms like a parent teacher night, my father was legally deaf. All the air was then sucked out of the room and my stature diminished smaller then a bug.

She continued to say that he wasn't completely deaf but legally deaf meaning his hearing was too impaired and had to be classified as disabled.

Ok… Stop… Hold on… This doesn't make any sense that my father was deaf because I carried conversations with my father he has never used sign language, when going to his job he talks with his coworkers and laughs at their jokes. When walking the street, as popular as he was, carried conversations with everybody he knew speaking back in a clear enough language that we all understood.

So at what point am I supposed to see that my father was deaf? My mom goes on to say that my father fought against the odds and his struggle with hearing by teaching himself to read lips and obviously taught himself so well that he functioned as a person that had perfect hearing. When talking with someone she said he would stare on a persons lips and not their face to prepare himself to have the appropriate response. I then had a flashback of all my conversations and moments of laughter with my dad and can honestly say that every time I talked with him he was staring at my lips. When at his job and he spoke to his boss he would be so intense focusing on each persons lips. She asked me why didn't I know that, my answer was because he always answered people when talking to them, and laughed at jokes at the correct time, how could I have known without someone telling me.

Then she began to run down the list of how my father was always a worker from his youth, working on a milk truck getting up at 4am to start his day to working at a jewelry store and always held down a job and was good at it. Even though the doctor report stated that my dad was born with poor hearing. His mother, my grandmother, bought him two hearing aids and he didn't like either of them.

My dad told them the hearing aid made a loud piercing sound and he didn't like it and would always throw them away. He still did not get deterred from his commitments in life. Then my mom goes on to tell me that regardless of this struggle and change of life that this is why my dad taught himself how to read lips. My mom said that since the age of twelve he taught himself so well that he functioned at home, on his jobs, and in our town as a person without a disability. I said to myself at this point, this couldn't be the same person that I'm mad at. My mom opened my eyes to see my father for who he really was but by this time I took a second look at my dad he had colon cancer battling for his life. Struggling everyday, needing to be washed by my mother, some days of which I had to help her get him in and out of the shower. I was there to bring her the folding chair for him to sit in the shower so she could bathe him, I was there when my mom had to use a turkey baster and squeeze water into his rectum in order for my dad to defecate because he became very constipated due to his sickness. I was there when she had to help him in and out of the bed. In these moments I had a lot of conversations with my dad, some of which resulted in him coming to here me preach.

    I had to reevaluate my life because the person who I thought was not there in my life the way I needed, became "THE" greatest inspiration in my life. Here I was looking for something to motivate me to come out of what caused my depression and to push me to never give up on life, to fill that void in my life. In my prayers when I asked God to fill this void in my life and take away this emptiness, in response from God it was not some mystical moment but I received my answer when God opened my eyes to see my dad. So now I remember all the times my dad was there, I remembered he was there when I graduated college in 2003 and was there to see my first girl friend that now is my wife. Knowing how he lived his life and the struggles he endured putting me in a place of humility that this person was my Dad. These were now my thoughts looking down into his casket. It breaks my heart and remains to be a consistent heartache that I had to bury my dad on June 28th, which is my birthday. I felt like I lost my best friend, I felt like I could have gotten so much more out of life had I known who he really was. He is my reason I never give up, the reason I push myself to be a better father. June 28th 2004 my father became my HERO!

I. AM. DAD. _____

There was one point in my life where I never thought I would be a father, it seemed like I was going to be single forever. I was never a player, one that had multiple girlfriends, or one that was too hot to trot. I was extremely to myself, to where people in my family questioned whether or not I would ever be with somebody. I didn't even start dating until I was in college and that was only because I felt I was getting too old to have never even tried to at least talk to girls. It's not like God was going to drop a wife right in my face, I have to be able to communicate with females if I expect to marry a girl one day. There are plenty of people not married and having children in the world, the process of me wanting to get married first then have children is more from what I believe then how some choose to start their family. I never explored these facts until I started two years after getting to college in 1998 and this is why people never expected me to have children before marriage or after. There was a low expectation for me to even get a girlfriend let alone get married because I dated my first legit girlfriend in 2003.

Nevertheless, it may have been a long wait after dating three times, my third date became my wife and not to long after she was pregnant with our first child.

After all this time of waiting, holding out, and doing our best to stay true to our beliefs, my first experience as a dad ended up being a horrible one. There weren't a lot of heavy preparations for the baby to come home like being set with a baby shower but we were using our newlywed mentality of just going with the flow. We were on the high of being newly married, having our first apartment, and now having our first baby. Doctor visits were a regular but this particular time going in for a routine checkup changed my entire experience as a father. My wife was about twenty-two weeks pregnant at the time of this visit but the nurses were acting very strange during this visit. They would come in and check her then whisper to each other then leave the room, repeating this a few times to where we began to get weary of the wait. We were tired and ready to go home but it was like we were being held hostage, then after such a long wait we find out that her pressure was high and they were running additional test to see how to get this under control. Before we knew it doctors came out to us to say that she cannot go home because her pressure was extremely high, I believe it was 225 over 125.

I totally understand the precaution from the doctor's perspective because my wife was in hypertension stage 3. Hypertension stage 3 is the most severe form of high blood pressure, when your systolic value is over 180 and your diastolic value is over 110 mmHg. But regardless of her issues with her pressure there were no signs of high blood pressure. My wife had no symptoms of faint, vomiting, or dizziness and felt like we should have been ok to go home.

She thought a prescription for some

high blood pressure pills should do the trick and we could go home. To my surprise, shortly after that thought I found myself driving behind an ambulance heading to another doctor who specializes in high risk pregnancies, Dr. David L. Principe, MD. I am really trying to understand what am I dealing with right now, I'm praying and asking God for wisdom. Once we get to our destination we sat again for hours, after which I became restless and needed some clear answers to why are we going through these charades until 3am. In comes the Doctor, the specialist, he first told us the obvious that my wife has extremely high blood pressure. Which we already knew but we continued to tell him that she feels great so why can't we go home? Then Doctor Principe took his time and explained the incredible danger that my wife was in due to this high pressure.

He explained that the cause of the high blood pressure was a result of high levels of protein in her urine and that my wife had developed something called *Preeclampsia.*

Preeclampsia *(pre-e-CLAMP-si-a) is a condition unique to human pregnancy. It is diagnosed by the elevation of the expectant mother's blood pressure usually after the 20th week of pregnancy. Preeclampsia is to be diagnosed by persistent high blood pressure that develops during pregnancy or the postpartum period that is associated with high levels of protein in the urine* **OR** *the new development of decreased blood platelets, trouble with the kidneys or* *liver, fluid in the lungs, or signs of brain trouble such as seizures and/or visual disturbances. http://bit.do/preeclampsiaor (preeclampsia.com)*

In my wife's case the first signs of persistent high blood pressure was evident and the stages only looked to worsen. He continued, by telling us that the child was healthy but my wife was not and that this issue threatened the life of my wife and would put our child at risk for proper development. She was not expected to carry full term in good health. The doctor then stops everything… Looks at us… and gives an unbelievable ultimatum.

He told us that we had to make a choice, to put my wife's life at risk and continue with the pregnancy or terminate the pregnancy. What type of choice is this for a first time dad? What type of choice am I supposed to make here? I want my baby and I want my wife! But I'm being told that I cannot have both. Here is my first opportunity to be a dad and I felt like this doctor was telling me to kill my child. This was my opportunity to finally have a child call me dad and it was being snatched from me. After much deliberation, consideration, and prayer we made the choice to let the child go. We went through all the necessary preparations for this procedure, which required that they induce her labor and she would push the baby out. MY BABY GIRL... I held her in my hands she was so small. Unfortunately, we had to deal with some resident doctors who will go nameless because a few of them were so heartless trying to speed along this process like my wife was supposed to push the baby out then they take her and just dispose of her in a garbage bag. My wife had yelled a few times to kick them out of the room.

    Dr. Principe was like a saving grace during these moments due to his respect level around the hospital. The face of these resident doctors that I had to watch while my wife was trying to make the best of a bad situation.

She wanted to get clothes for the baby, and she wanted us to take pictures with the baby trying to make the moment feel like she was alive. But regardless of these inconsiderate moments, when I held my daughter for the first time after she had just come out and I said "hello", she opened her eyes and looked at me. I don't really care what anybody says, I felt like she knew who I was, and I felt like she knew my voice from all the times I talked to her in the belly. When I spoke to her and she opened her eyes I felt like she knew I was her dad.

I will keep that moment for the rest of my life…

There were many people we looked to for guidance that were not there, many that we looked to for advice before making this decision and proved to be of no support. Truthfully, even with that hardship we do not point any fingers at anybody because it didn't add or take away from the situation. God is always in control and He saw fit to let life take its course and brought our baby home with Him. We will always miss our daughter, we still miss her everyday so much that after we buried her and yes we had a small funeral, just Eboné, and me we have not been back to see her grave yet because it still hurts.

We have moved on but there is just this thought of wanting it all to have been successful and we brought our baby home.

I love my little girl, she recognized my voice, and she opened her eyes to see me... *That's what I believe.*

Here I am years later and my wife Eboné has accomplished some great goals in life as regards to weight loss pushing her to new limits. I think it was three years before we tried to have another child and the question now is do I see myself as a father? She gave birth to our son Jaxon Martin Steward July 12,

2013 and February 11, 2015 she gave birth to our daughter Violette Ebonae Steward. Coming into the first pregnancy we had a fear of the 22 weeks, not having any of the same health issues like the first but then coming into the 22nd week just flooded back all the memories. Even though it was years later it still felt like yesterday but we got past the 22 weeks, and she carried full term. Once my son was born, did I see myself as a father? No, it was more like a dream.

I would soon have someone call me dad, I wasn't really sure how I would measure up as a dad but I knew I was bringing my child home, I was by no means going to bury another child neither was I going to lose my wife.

I didn't care about any doctor's report or

anything people had to say, I was not going to bury another child. Now having a son and then my daughter shortly after this is no longer a dream, Martin has kids. The different challenges that we faced together mentally, physically, financially, and emotionally, I needed to be there for my wife. She faced many challenges as a wife, as a mother to be and I was with her every second of the day. I tried to lean on that quality and utilize that strength to help me be a father. Here it is we were bringing home a baby boy then two years later we brought home our baby girl. After all of these great moments happening in my family, did I see myself as dad yet? No. But ready or not, I'm dad. My initial feelings once my children were home threw me off; it was a reality check that playtime was over. Everything that I had as a methodology for parenting was now on the table, this was no longer a conversation about parenting but it was instead time to be a parent. Thoughts were running through my head in regards to me being adequate enough for parenting especially as a parent of two kids. The one thing that really pushed me almost over the edge was the sleep pattern of every two hours needing food and when my daughter would wake up crying for food it woke my son up every time.

Due to the need of rest for my wife coming home after a C-Section operation I refused to ask for help while managing my two kids every night untll my wife was back to herself. This was to prove to myself that I am able to be who my children and my wife need me to be. Now this was no easy task, our son was a holler head even though my wife may disagree but when Jaxon first came home he would let you know he was hungry. He would not stop screaming until he was fed and put back to sleep. He would scream like he fell on the floor and nobody came to help, I mean He would scream bloody murder and almost immediately after his bottle he would go right to sleep. This was consistent every night, seemingly never ending and then when my daughter Violette came into this picture I truthfully some nights felt like I would lose my mind.

    However, regardless of the difficulty I took this as my personal responsibility because I needed to be their father. I had to give up the concept of not being good enough and just be enough. Anything I didn't know just meant I had to learn, some things I had to YouTube, even Google. You have to be willing to learn what you do not know, even though I would say that I have learned a lot in my lifetime about taking care of kids from babysitting.

Babysitting in my teen years was like almost having a child, with my dad out to work and my mom working as a home health aid and having to stay in her clients home a week before she comes back home for the weekend. While she was away and my dad working all day my little nieces and nephews that lived with us needed to go to school, needed to eat, needed to be washed, etc. I've had my share of time spent learning how to manage behaviors, change diapers, and feeding kids, learning most from my brother Fred. Now being a dad to my own children is a whole different ball game, I had to learn how to make bottles fast, memorize the measurements for the powdered milk so it could be done in the dark, training my body to wake up when they cry or hear them when they fall. I soon learned I had a benefit with my kids that when they cried for food it was because that was all they needed to calm down. They both could sleep through the night with a full stomach, even though there was so many theatrics before a full stomach I learned to count my blessings. My kids would go through subtle stages that required small amounts of consistent assistance in a particular area that actually would always satisfy their needs.

I first noticed these stages or patterns first with my son, that instead of calling them episodes I called them stages.

My son Jaxon, when having a crying fit I knew that he was tired but he wouldn't just go to sleep he would have a fit first. I would pat him on his butt, walk around the dining room table before he would go to sleep, I'm guessing the movement helped him go to sleep. Then two weeks after none of those strategies didn't work for sleep it became the rocking chair and patting on the butt. Some weeks after this it was the strategy of the daddy grip, which was simply having my child gripped in the cuff of my arm with their head comfortably cradled between my bicep and forearm combined with a few minutes of walking and both my kids couldn't stay awake. They would fall asleep in a matter of 15 minutes. Those were the good days. What I've noticed was that these strategies revealed a lot of the characteristics of who my child would become. Because I was attacking what stressed my child the most to put them to sleep therefore I paid close attention to them learning their most disrupting attributes. This revelation gave me the opportunity to focus my attention on correcting these troubling characteristics.

As I continued this journey I noticed my wife and I were the epitome of the LUV's first time parent commercial. Taking every possible precaution when dealing with our first child and soon as the second came the whole dynamic of our house changed.

We weren't as nervous or fearful any longer. During this whole process we saw so many different stages of development for the better, thank God.

Now, at these young ages, just a couple of months old for each of our kids another stage of development came up where our children started playing my wife and I against each other. For my son, it seemed very odd how he would always cry at specific times when my wife would pass the room to give him more of what I already gave him, as to say mommy will get me what I want when I cry at this octave. My son understood how to get picked up when it is time to go to bed or eat more after the first setting. My daughter was a little more laid back and has a great sleeping pattern but only demonstrated this behavior for food and to be picked up. Now, this behavior started in the house and eventually worked its way outside of the house in Wal-Mart, Shoprite, the Shopping Mall, etc. Once this started, as the dad I had to consider another form of development of parenthood that needed to be constructed firmly in our family, the institution of DISCIPLINE. Whether in the house, outside of the house, or making decisions I remain as the dad. My wife and I are both working parents, but do I keep a title as dad if I'm not living up to it? How do I keep the title as dad if I'm not bringing money home to support my family?

Do I keep the title as Dad if I allow my wife to do all the parenting and I only step in to make corrections? Do I keep the title as Dad if I only throw money your way for child support but never spend time with you? I didn't see myself as a dad if I didn't have an active role in all stages of their development. I do not believe the wife managing the kids only and I go make the money. I wanted my kids to have more of me.

Some people want a home where the wife does all the cooking, cleaning and taking care of the kids but I never wanted that in my home. I love to see my wife active in the world, in business, and in her career. No she can't do everything and even if she could do all or be all around the house, I won't let her! I am Mr. Fix it, I do the dirty work, I change tires, I made it my business to learn how to put my kids to sleep, I do the dishes (mainly because I don't cook). I mean I can cook (spaghetti) and I have a mean handle on... cold cereal, but real cooking I leave that solely to my wife. She can put a hurting on the pots and pans. Now if she's not feeling well or not home I'll throw something together only because this to me is dad. Dad has to make the hard decisions, parental decisions, and even final decisions. As dad, I also believe I have developed the skill of not just listening to my wife but the skill of knowing "when" to listen to my wife.

My wife Eboné is full of ideas and suggestions that is sure to produce in anything that she puts her mind too but this isn't a one sided relationship. Our children need both of us and this is why for decisions I don't always go with my wife's choice I'll go with some of mine because our kids need to see that I am here. I don't have to be haled as king and we only do things my way but on the right occasion we need to see things going daddy's way. The greatest moment for me as dad is when my way seemed impossible and not believable and wouldn't you know it my way worked out above all. The best example was when I saw my daughter putting a foreign object into her mouth and I worked with her to understand that she cannot do this, that she needed to spit it out. It took a little time but eventually she understood, then two days later I over heard my wife talking to her trying to get her to open her mouth and let out another foreign object. I sat and listened for a minute and considered she will eventually get her to do so. Should I wait, or use the way and phrases I used that prompted her to let it out? I chose my way just in case it could turn for the worse and jumped up walked up to my daughter, put my open hand in front of her mouth and said, "Violette… Out!" and immediately she started spitting the object out.

 My wife hollered in amazement and said I quit that's it, how did you do that. I tried to explain what I did just a few days before but she was laughing too hard to hear and was in awe of my daddy moment. That was a good day for me. Now of course, when her way is the better way of doing a thing or handling a situation we will do it her way. But these choices create balance for me as dad. Sometimes when managing our children I'll take my wife's concept of how it should be done and do it better then she would, this stands true still today as making me a better dad when knowing when to listen to my wife. Spending time, money and energy, on my kids has been the greatest investment for me as dad. If there isn't anything I don't know I ask God for wisdom, I pray to keep my head on straight. I believe in prayer and that it is the reason for all my success that I have gained as a dad. My relationship with God has stood strong. I could not take the credit for my acceleration as trying to be a good dad.

I've learned to take parenting like a puzzle and that regardless of the pieces broken in the box you have a guarantee that they can be put together just so long as you have the patience to put these pieces together you will succeed. With my love for puzzles I've learned to enjoy putting these pieces together, pieces like learning what will make "My" family function better.

Some dads live their lives like their family is better without them but I never intended to have a family like that, I didn't want baby mama drama, I didn't want to just see my kids on the weekend, I wanted to always be involved in the lives of my children. Furthermore, I always wanted to be in my wife's life, I want to be her conqueror, I want to be her knight in shinning armor, I take the challenge no matter how hard it gets. I accept the challenge of putting the pieces together and how to make it work getting to see the full puzzle. Because not only am I dad for my children but I am also dad for my wife as well, why do I say this because I've seen it in action ever time I do something beneficial for my kids when it makes them happy, it keeps a smile on their face. It has nothing to do with spoiling them but just from the time that I spend with them the face that she has when I turn around is like I have become her knight in shinning armor. Because I am keeping the family happy or I am keeping the family together.

These are priceless moments when I am dad to my children it keeps the love in my home which is to say that I am not just in my house as a husband or just as her man but I am dad. When something brakes around the house dad has it, when we needed the refrigerator to get upstairs... dad can do it, when we needed the dishwasher to be put up and installed... dad has it.

Why is it dad that has it, because while I'm working or fixing something and my kids try to get in the mix I incorporate them somehow in the job. When I allow these moments of teaching, to me, I have successfully switched gears to being a dad. I will shield them from danger to ensure the opportunity to teach my kids and have that moment as a dad. Unless it is way too dangerous but I'll take the extra precaution to allow my kids to help me and create this daddy moment. If I am doing handy man things around the house I'll call for my son to help me, not needing his help because he's just a baby but to see him use his little muscles and him feeling like he just saved my life was a moment worth my time. I don't like to leave my kids to always stay sitting and watching TV or playing video games, no it is imperative that they spend time with me because in the eyes of my children and my wife I. Am. Dad. Sometimes, even as a dad you have to be willing to reinvent yourself. You talk about so many celebrities that use the strategy of reinventing oneself when their career is struggling or if they need to change the perception of themselves in the eyes of people. They figure out a way to reinvent their identity so they can move on to better their career. The responsibility as a dad should be taken just as serious.

When you feel like you are struggling as a dad it is imperative that you reinvent yourself as a dad in the lives of your children and as a great dad in front of your wife.

If I can quote TD Jakes, "You can go through drama on your job, in your neighborhood, or even your church but you should be able to come home to peace. This is where you live, where you lay your head, after a stressful day this is supposed to be your place of solitude." How then do you expect peace in your home when your wife or another man is fulfilling your role as the man? Well I have made it my business as I told my wife that I am willing to work for my peace. The revelation of my assignment came from *Genesis 1:1, "In the beginning God created the heavens and the earth"*. The part that was relevant to me reinventing myself was the beginning portion of that verse, "In the beginning God created". This is to understand that every human being has the ability to tap into his or her creative nature when you start a new beginning. This may be for some to start a new business, have a new family, or saying I Do to your wife on your wedding day, etc. Start something new! For me, my beginning was the commitment to being a good dad, even a great dad.

The start of my journey as a dad was scary being unsure of how am I going make out as a father, just as the scripture said that the earth was dark and void. But from this dark place God committed to starting something new and his creative nature poured out of Him. Having children was my new beginning, I was scared, I didn't know how I would turn out in their lives but regardless of this dark place I've committed myself to my new beginning and from this I am seeing my creativity rise. I want to be undeniable, I want this to be unmistakable, and I want to be irreplaceable to my wife, my children, and anyone who knows me that I. AM. DAD.

DISCIPLINE _____

Now that I've touched so many areas of fatherhood, I have to touch on this next subject that is so delicate and it is discipline. Everyone has their own philosophy on how to discipline their child and having their own means to raise their children. I have developed my own philosophy as well and for me it works. Not just for my own children but it has worked while I would babysit my nieces and nephews, then there were summer camps, etc. Of course starting out using my strategies on other children I could say that it worked but you cannot be sure until you have your own. Using these methods now in my own home, so far they have been beneficial. First question that must be answered is, do I believe in discipline? YES.

Who is the disciplinarian in our home? We both are disciplinarians. We both agree that to keep some type of structure in the house that discipline will establish some order. Who takes the reigns when trying to stay true to the order that we set in the house? For example; if Mommy or Daddy said so... Then it must be done... That is me. Yes the quiet introvert is a belligerent disciplinarian and I would not say that it is my way or the highway, where one could not tie their shoe without my consent.

No, it's not nearly that bad but more toward what is intended on being taught to my child, I am firm in that I mean what I say. The next question that comes up when discussing discipline is do you "beat" your child, which always leans right into child abuse where the parent doesn't feel comfortable correcting his or her own child. In many ways it is not all due to the government trying to take over how we raise our kids because parents, father's to be precise, have lost the know how when disciplining their children. In this age of technology it has made the responsibility of fatherhood very hard and this is without taking into consideration the issues a father undertakes with his children's mother whether she is his wife or not, being a dad is not an easy job. How to correct your child is a very touchy subject, so I am going to jump in this touchy subject right away... Do I believe in beating my children? Is beating your children a correct form of discipline and are we bringing this into our new family?

Well lets set the record straight that I have coined my own definition in this area of discipline, where I must describe the difference between beating your child verses spanking your child. Some would argue that beating your child and spanking are the same but I beg to differ mainly because it fits in my philosophy in regards to disciplining a child.

This being one of the tools to help discipline your child when it concerns correction, understanding of course that spanking is not the only way you are supposed to discipline your child. The way that I approach beating a child started initially from my influence in the church and learning scripture being that I started out in the church so young at thirteen years of age.

In biblical scriptures it tells me that there is nothing wrong with the rod of correction *(Proverbs 22:15)* or where it says if you beat your child he will not die but you will deliver his soul from Hell *(Proverbs 23:13-14)*. These scriptures are commonly used when referring to disciplining your child in the form of beating them but has it been used out of content, being used as a crutch instead of doing what you really need to do. Now lets breakdown this philosophy of beating your child verses spanking your child, according to my definition from my experience in fatherhood. Beating a child is similar to the same actions of someone that unleashes an unmeasured amount of aggression towards an individual they dislike. This aggression is normal when a person is in a fight and you end up hurting this individual. There is no way you can tell me that it is appropriate or good parenting in this situation where you may hurt your child.

Then someone says, when I say that I beat my child I am not talking about hurting my child but I only intend on correcting my child. Well if the object of this method of discipline where one would beat their child is intended for correction, now that we see the aggressive nature that comes behind the act of beating, lets challenge this approach by considering the concept of spanking your child. We must first go back to the scripture where I originated from and understand that the meaning of the rod of correction is referring to something of sufficient strength being used when bringing correction.

This object of sufficient strength is not talking about ironing cords, the shoe, or the flip-flop wedged on the side of the bed that was grabbed and launched at the child because the parent is annoyed with their child's disobedience but does not feel like getting up to correct them. This approach to discipline I labeled as beating your child where all of the attention is more focused on letting out your aggravation with the child and not enough attention being applied to teaching the child to understand. We focus so much on the wording of the scripture when it says to beat your child and not a consistent view on the purpose of the child learning.

In every occasion where the scripture says to correct your child the primary focus was always to learn from the correction and not to break the established laws in the house that have the purpose of benefiting the whole house not to support the laziness of a parent. So what I have done to help me comprehend the purpose of learning gained when following the scripture I don't use the term beating my child but I spank my children with the primary purpose of teaching my children. As far as changing the terminology, I have also adjusted that where I often don't tell my children they are going to get a spanking but rather I say, "YOU NEED HELP". I normally place it in question form and tell my children, "Excuse me... Do you need some HELP?"

This was crucial when my kids came into the stages of challenging me as a father and when I initiate the order in the home that I Am Dad.

There will be conflict but how do I deal with conflict from a three year old and a one year old? According to my experiments I offer some HELP... This is when I set the boundary of informing my child at that moment to stop your actions and redirect your anger or frustration and bring them to an end. Then I can see when my child is mentally trying to figure if they should leave the situation alone or challenge my authority and of course in the beginning stages they often choose to challenge my authority.

Now if my child has pushed me to a high level of frustration in their disobedience because I repeatedly told them not to do a certain thing, especially if it's something that will hurt them, in this situation beating my child is not an option. Why is this, because whenever anything is done out of frustration or anger you carry large amounts of adrenalin. Typically when you move or act through adrenalin you move faster, hit harder because you are reacting from a subconscious built up emotion. How do you see it to be ok to unleash this anger on your child, where often times from these reactions the child ends up having whelp marks or bruises. I consider this to be beating your child when it comes from the place of frustration and anger not following the true meaning of the scriptures as aforementioned, if you follow the teaching of the proverbs. But I do believe in and agree with spanking your child but what is the biggest difference? Beating your child comes from a place of anger and spanking your child comes from wanting to teach your child. Someone then says, "When I beat my kid, I am teaching them... I'm teaching them a lesson."

Here's where I settled my difference between the two, you may feel you're teaching when beating your child while you are frustrated but is the child learning? You are so focused on getting out your anger that you fail to attend to the greater need, which is the opportunity to train your child's mind. This cannot happen being birthed out of anger, therefore if I am angered by my child's actions I actually choose to go cool off or let my wife handle it, as I am not in position at that time to teach. On the same hand, if I stop being lazy when my children are having behavioral issues and choose to correct their actions before I'm frustrated and choose to use the method of spanking my child to the level that satisfies their behavior, which may only be two or three pops on the backside, I feel I am in complete ordinance with what I believe in and even in compliance with governmental law that this is not child abuse. My final analysis of this subject is that this is just one method of disciplining my children not the only method. As a father to my children, they should hear my voice more often then just in correction or only receiving praise when prompted by my wife. No, I believe you are well aware of your role as a father when more then just your child's negative behavior draws your attention. I am well aware that speaking to my children can bring correction, a time out (age appropriate) will bring correction, bringing the attention of my child to what they have done wrong will also bring correction.

If they need a little extra help then they may have to get a spank, as I say it to my kids. It's only one of the methods of correction and not to be focused on as the greatest teaching tool.

We are living in a different day where we can't get away with saying how our parents put sport on our backside and we turned out ok. Different era, better tools for discipline. I also believe that if you play your cards right, making this correction early in your child's life will warrant more verbal correction with positive results rather then consistent physical correction and worsening behavior.

    This I hope helped the understanding that the approach to correcting a child through discipline has to change. Using any available object to chastise your child is inappropriate and wrong but using a simple belt strap or an open hand on the backside of your child while you are in a calm state of mind I believe is sufficient for correction. Being well aware that this method of correction is only available if you have exhausted all verbal de-escalation techniques and warnings. Staying under control is the primary focus for discipline because this allows you to issue understanding for what you are trying to help them learn.

My son Jaxon was showing great signs of advancement when he started walking and talking, he was picking up on so many skills as a developing child. This gave me the thought to start teaching him boundaries outside and how to stay close to me while walking. I also aided him in learning how to never lose sight of his mother or myself while he is walking. Then there is the amazing racetrack of cars or what we call the street. This is to teach him that cars hurt and we must stop at however many feet away from the curb until I get to you. Which are only a few steps away but nonetheless, it is to teach him to stop by my voice.

This is crucial in all areas of discipline, that your child knows your voice, they know tonal changes of what tone of voice means. They know the tone of voice for when you're happy verses what tone of voice means you're upset. Again, I will emphasize that none of these disciplinary actions are to satisfy a parents laziness to instruct your child while they are learning right from wrong or to bring comfort to a parent's aggravated day. As an artist/ graphic designer I think of my kids as a blank canvas, a new document, an unshaped pod of clay that needs molding, completely innocent, a new hard drive, a new mind. Do not take such a blessed opportunity of receiving this new mind and download hatred into it or prejudice or low self worth, and etcetera.

Discipline should be viewed as discipleship.

Train up a child in the way that they should go so when they are old they will not depart. —Proverbs 22:6

Now let me give the meaning: Train up a *mind* in the way that they should go so when they are old they will not depart.

At what age should you begin discipleship or using discipline with your child? Without going into reasoning and age requirements how about we only place it with when the child has the ability to start making choices. Because we must touch on the subject of your child's ability to grasp what you intend to teach them, or is your child's brain developing correctly.

Some parents find themselves in denial when it comes to their child and if their brain is developing correctly or does my child have a deficiency. We live in a society of labels being placed on kids as early as two and three years of age but I am not associating a label on any child. I am just being mindful of parents disciplinary action towards a child that is not able to grasp the information as fast as a normal pace developed mind. Without applying a label can we at least be honest when a child needs more time, more patience and more love towards their need to learn. Understanding this fact that just because a child processes information slower then most does not mean they cannot write their own book one day. Just because a child processes information slower then most does not mean they cannot be a gifted graphic designer. Just because a child processes information slower then most does not mean he or she cannot be an excellent father. All of the above are some of my struggles and I have excelled in all, and yes it has taken me longer then most to get the job done but the job was done well, I am very proud of it. If you can be honest about your child's development they will be awarded the opportunity to grow into what this world needs to succeed. On the other hand, if you ignore these signs and remain in denial and choose to discipline your child without taking into consideration their need for added patience and time to comprehend then to me that should be considered child abuse. Taking into consideration what is measured as child abuse in the eyes of the U.S. Department of Health.

According to the Joyful Heart Foundations website: http://www.joyfulheartfoundation.org/learn/child-abuse-neglect/about-issue

Child abuse is defined as any recent act or failure to act on that results in a child's serious physical or emotional harm, sexual abuse, exploitation or death. An act or failure to act that presents a risk of serious harm to a child is also considered to be child abuse.

Each state provides its own definitions of child abuse within civil and criminal statutes, but they are informed by the following definitions of various forms of child abuse:

- **Physical.** A non-accidental physical injury as a result of punching, beating, kicking, biting,

shaking, throwing, stabbing, choking, hitting, burning or otherwise harming a child, that is inflicted by a parent, caregiver or other person who has responsibility for the child. Such injury is considered abuse regardless of whether the caregiver intended to hurt the child.
- **Sexual.** A form of child abuse that includes any sexual act performed with a child by an adult or older child, with or without force or threat of force. It may start as seemingly innocent touching and progress to more serious acts, including verbal seduction or abuse, anal or vaginal intercourse, oral sex, sodomy, manual stimulation, direct threats, implied threats or other forms of abuse.

- **Emotional.** A pattern of behavior that impairs a child's emotional development or sense of self-worth. This form of abuse is almost always present when other forms of abuse are identified.
It may include constant criticism, threats or rejection, as well as withholding love, support or guidance. Emotional abuse is often difficult to prove and, therefore, Child Protective services may not be able to intervene without clear evidence of harm to the child.
- **Psychological.** This is a pattern of behavior that affects a child's sense of worth by communicating to the child that he or she is not worthy, loved or important. Psychological abuse may include harsh demands, constant criticism, threats and

yelling. Witnessing other violent incidents such as, domestic violence or school violence is also a form of psychological abuse due to the intense fear it produces and the indirect threat to a child's safety.

Truthfully, even with these serious laws that are strictly enforced by the government, most parents still make up there own means of disciplinary actions for there children. Mainly because the government doesn't monitor our homes and every action of neither the good parent or the poorly performing parent but it is left to each parent to choose to love and raise their children to benefit society, even the world.

This is why I stress using discipline as a means of training a child and not condemning a child in their early stages. As the adage goes, "You must bend the tree while they are young and still tender (bendable)". This being understood, you of course need to understand that spanking your child is the last resort when training your child in their behavior, there are other effective methods always referred to when disciplining your child.

1. Time out
2. Ignoring
3. Stern speech or verbal warning
4. Picking your battles

Time Out to me is very effective after a child understands what a spanking means and also has a passion for particular liberties around the house.

So when the parent says they are in time out it is understood that they avoided the spanking becauseit isn't needed but I have to lose watching PJ Mask or Mickey Mouse Clubhouse, which are some of my son's favorite TV shows.

Ignoring is effective when your child understands how to get over on you or playing parents against each other. For example, my son knows when he is with me whining will not get him an ice cream before dinner, so he would have to shut down and do what is expected of him. But sometimes when mommy comes around he understands that if he reaches a certain octave in his cry that mommy will forget about the order we established in the house and deal with the crises at hand, which is the need for peace and quiet.

Stern Speech or Verbal Warning is the effort to avoid yelling at your child. Tonal control for me as Dad is crucial because there is a major difference when mom speaks verses when Dad speaks. This of course is if Dad has his role as the disciplinarian in the house and a dominant figure in the child's life. I do not agree with cursing at your child, furthermore I do not agree with embarrassing your child. To me it only makes the parent look foolish, childish and having no control.

Picking Your Battles has been the greatest blessing for my wife and I. It helped us come to grips with knowing that we are doing a good job as parents and every misbehaving action by our children does not have to result in a disciplinary response from any of these methods. We would just look at each other and say, "Babe pick your battles". In other words, every **action** doesn't require a **reaction**.

Sometimes you have to pick the times you deem it necessary to discipline your child and other times you just need to move on with your day.

Learn to pick your battles.

I must also touch on the aspect of how a child will process information, as this is something that I had to deal with growing up. Due to the issue of children being labeled I just want men to understand how our active role will help in our children's development regardless of their struggles. Every father that is active in their child's life must understand what crosses the thin line into child abuse because active parenthood from dad will benefit the development of the child's life.

I stand by this position after evaluating my children's response to my active role in their lives. My first born, my son, I learned a lot from because I had to come to grips with his development. Of course I would not put a label on my son as having some kind of disorder.

However, when I go through all my methods of discipline and what I am trying to teach him is not registering then I must at least take another option into consideration. I had to be honest with myself that my son is an active child needing added patience and a little more time on certain matters. I know what this looks like all too well after working ten years in an environment for children with behavioral disorders, where I have seen how certain things can trigger them to carry out in a disorderly fashion. One of the ways I've learned to deescalate my sons hyper behavior is to speak very closely to his face. **Close proximity** with a calm, almost whispering tone of voice I give my son direction and boundaries. The boundaries of course are from the strategies of discipline; Time out, Ignoring, Verbal Warning, Picking My Battle, or The Spank. The close proximity in some kind of way breaks through the chaos in my sons mind at that moment bringing him back to listening and learning from me.

This is the way I learned how to understand the distress of a child in crisis:

A child in crisis mode | A child with peace of mind

Children in crisis mode having an episode believe it or not are looking for someone to help them come back to a peaceful state of mind. Some parents look to always make the child find their own way out of what looks like the crisis mode ball and its almost impossible by themselves. I have used my strategies on my children and even when working with children labeled with behavioral disorders and learning disorders. Each time at least one of my strategies worked to unravel the mind of that child in crisis into a mind of peace. As a father, I felt it necessary to be that solid circle and bring peace. You have to understand that we are dealing with children from a different era from the times any parent 30 years old and above grew up in.

Some parents believe they can discipline their children however they deem necessary. This is why children in this era are setting up phones in the corner of their room Live Streaming their parent on social media demonstrating all kinds of brutal discipline. My strategies not only effectively help me as a father but these strategies would not get anyone in trouble if seen on social media.

These were all my moments of learning as a father and needing to answer my one question of, how am I supposed to be a good father? When I was growing up the term, "It takes a village" went a long way. When a child got in trouble at school they first was reprimanded by the principal, shortly after this same child would almost get home when a neighbor saw them outside, knew about the problems in school and the neighbor would then chastise the child. Then when the parents finally came face to face with their children the parents gave the final judgment. That time of how families connected to help with children is extinct. Technology has allowed the child to gain the upper hand in some cases and rightfully so in many homes because some children in my day had it so ruff growing up, and the hardship that some parents put their children through was unnecessary. However, I do not desire to lose my place as Dad because I'm fearful of the worldview on how I ought to raise our children.

    The era that we live in now proves that if a parent fails to teach their child about the different dangers in substance abuse, sex, or cyber threats the Internet via social media and search engines have provides some type of an answer to satisfy the child's need to know. I am convinced that various ills that attack our youth can be handled better when they have active parents in their lives while they are still young – "Bend the tree while they are still tender". This is why I have provided myself with these different tools to aid in my parenting as a father. At this point I did not have a derivative to at least aid in my learning as a father. I did not know what to call my style of parenting I just knew it was hard and I knew as a parent I had to progress. I cannot be afraid to be a father to my own children, to be the father that is required in their lives. It is not only important but it is imperative that my position as a Dad is established in my child's life while they are young, even though many father's find themselves needing to make up for the lack of time sown in their child's life. But if you are blessed to have the opportunity of being in the seed stage of a child's life, understand that this information is how I took advantage of it. You can look at it two ways from the seed stage that of being when the child is physically a new born and you're in their life or if they are older but your relationship with them is newly born.

This could be possible due to your absence yet they have allowed you in their life... Please take advantage of the seed stage! I found myself fighting denial and trying not to believe that my child needs this type of attention but I would be a fool to resist this opportunity to better my child's development by understanding how to discipline.

Some may have heard the term, "Do as I say but not as I do" and if you haven't heard it you may have lived through it. You may also claim it to be true but it doesn't work if you want your child to follow your instructions as a Dad. It is only comprehendible if you are showing them how. In my house I make it my business to set the atmosphere to where everyone knows there is no cursing in my house, therefore there is no cursing when disciplining the children. I don't yell at my children but changing my tone of voice and stern warnings have been so affective. With my children in this matter I call it **"The Salty Sweet Mix"**. When one of my children are having an episode I speak very sternly with them, use one of my methods of discipline and if they don't snap out of their erratic mood they are in I use close proximity and soft speech right after the stern warning and for some reason they always calm down. The salty and sweet mix only works after a child has been introduced to all other methods of discipline.

Lastly, I had to determine who will be the dominant parent and which parent will enforce guidelines/ rules in my house. This however does not nullify the need of one parent over the other but rather it promotes both parents having to learn how to take the reigns in the house. Even though there is a dominant parent in respect to discipline, the responsibility of the dominant parent is to maintain honor from their children and to establish that same honor with the opposite parent. As a parent you want to avoid your children pinning you against one another to get what they want. Discipline is a combined effort and will only be effective when you reframe from laziness. Consistency in discipline during the beginning years of my children's life is how I expect to be successful and being committed to my methods of discipline is why I expect to conquer the fear of being an effective dad.

PROVIDER _____

Having the role as a provider, I must bring to your attention that every home is different but there is no reason that the mother in the house should go out to get the bacon, bring home the bacon, then after getting home make the bacon. Then after she feeds her family she cleans up the bacon and of course the end of this scenario is the husband is sitting home playing video games all day.

There is no excuse for any man with a family choosing not to provide for his family. Biblically speaking, Eve walked into a completed environment. Adam had already named the animals and the land had already been prepared so that when Eve first walked the earth she did not have to want for anything. If I may move forward into the era we live in now, life in the home is different when analyzing how one needs to provide for their family. Of course I will analyze my perspective toward how my family is provided for because both my wife and I must work full time jobs and this is just to make ends to meet. Thinking back to the times when we dated, who had the bigger paycheck switched hands quite often. Where at one point I made more then her, then she started working as a teacher some years after we were married and her salary tripled in comparison to mine. Does this remove me as being the provider in my home now that the salary of my wife trumps mine? How am I supposed to define myself as being a provider in my home?

I heard it this way, where a man told his wife he was going hunting for food so that the family can eat and he grabbed his gun then left. Not to long after he came home with a couple bullets in his gun, barely any sweat on his head and no catch. The husband walked through the door and said to his wife... I missed. That is an absolute joke to say that a man does not supply what the family needed, in this case being his sacrifice. It goes on to say that this man would have done better if after he had given his best shot to catch something for his family to eat but missed he then should have unloaded his gun, every shot, trying to hit his target. Once he unloaded and if he still missed he should have picked up his gun and threw it at his target. Then even if that missed he should have jumped up and chased his target, wrestling it to the ground. Even though he is returning home dirty, tired, hurt, and empty handed he at least can return home to say that he gave his everything to provide for his family, *-Bishop T.D. Jakes*.

When a man gives such a sacrifice consistently he will not continue to come up empty handed but it is inevitable for such efforts to produce provision even by merely the laws of sowing and reaping. On the same hand if one would reject the understanding of the biblical proverb that whatever a person sows they will reap then take it from the old adage: What goes around will surely come around. I simply understood this as a need to produce the tenacity for running after the provision for my family and that it would soon materialize in more ways than one. I do not personally take offense to my wife making more money then me at this present moment but I will not become comfortable in it either.

    Being a provider as a man for me is defined by my sacrifice not solely by my paycheck. It is noteworthy from how much time, energy, and money I expend to ensure that the needs of my family are met. It is necessary that I show action toward pursuing better, this is how I keep the stress level down for my wife. Due to the fact that I dissolve most of my issues internally, it becomes difficult for my wife to figure certain things out going on in my head. I still at specific intervals need to show some signs of life or some signs that I am moving forward. I don't have the wife that will be content being a housewife even though she will tell you different.

However, I know who I married and my wife is busy, mobile, energetic, full of life, and a hard worker – to say the least. Sometimes it feels like we both let out our fishhooks for advancement in this life with different bate or different personalities and the bate on my wife's hook seems to catch almost every time, big fish then small fish. What do I have to do to catch some fish to provide better for my family? I have really come to my wits end and so I've jumped in the water to catch some fish by any means necessary. I am pulling on every resource I have to see which one will help provide for my family, from every talent that God has given me: Graphic Design, Web Design, Illustrator, Author,

Aspiring Film Director, Playwright, Actor, Mentor, all around Handy Man, etc. I am about to even start a mobile barbershop if it helps because I cut hair like a professional. Something has to give but until it does I must keep grinding. As the provider, it also helps to have good credit believe it or not, I cannot tell you how many times I was in position to take out a loan from my employers credit union to manage bills and keep us functioning through the summer due to having July and August off. Paid all those loans off and continued my hustle for something more stable to help provide for my family.

This is just feeling like an up hill battle, and now after financial changes we haven't been able to keep payments for all our bills on time which sent our credit to an unlikely place. What am I to do when my wife cannot see the light at the end of the tunnel? Well I will tell you the beginning of what we did, we started to hold fast to the power of prayer and believe that God will fix this. Now this does not mean we are to sit and wait for something to fall out of Heaven but rather look for the answer in unlikely places. So now when a friend to my wife suggests that we go see a mortgage person about a house and when we go he tells us we are not in place to get the house yet but we should spend this time fixing our credit to better our chances of getting approved for a house. Then this same person lays out a plan that would help resolve our credit issues and put us on a much clearer path toward better during this transition, WOW!

Priceless information that I take as our answer from God that just requires for us to deal with the issues we face and work on them. To be disciplined in fixing my credit is a means of providing for my family, understanding again that being the provider is not just about the money but being a provider as a man for me is defined by my sacrifice not solely by my paycheck. It is noteworthy from how much time, energy, and money I expend to ensure that the needs of my family are met.

Fixing my credit falls in the category of time, energy and eventually money. I have to push, follow my strengths and believe God to make a way out of no way. I believe the same way seasons change naturally that life circumstances change as well. We are not intended to live in the valley for the rest of our lives I just have to remain consistent for when seasons change in my favor. I don't feel like I am degrading myself by working with any odd job and filtering what has the ability to bring provision for my family. I feel like I have the right to define how I provide for my family, it works for me. I'm not breaking the law to bring provision, going against any moral standards as an ordained Elder in my church, and it doesn't make me feel less than a man because of this route that I have to take for a possible means of provision. I am not in competition to see who make more in my home for me to feel like the man but when we aren't living paycheck to paycheck anymore is when I will feel better as the man in my home.

I want my wife and I to be in position to give to our church, pay our bills, save, put food in our home, open a new stream of income, and invest. Due to my continued push toward better I have made the attempt to take a leap of faith and leave my job to follow my dreams and push my gift in graphic design.

There wasn't anything wrong with my job but I just did not have opportunity to advance there, all of the necessary paperwork needed to attain better positions I did not have. With the way my brain is set up... Information is just moving to slow to get want is needed in this current job.

I cannot say I did not try, I spent money taking tests to gain new positions but I kept failing (7 times to be exact). I felt like I have exhausted all my options with this current job, this is why I left. Wanting to flow with the insight of Steve Harvey about taking a leap (Steve Harvey Show), my Pastor Jevah L. Richardson about removing the life jacket (Counseling), and even my Bishop Eric K. Clark about the seed only being able to become a tree once it removes the outer shell that kept it protected (Maximizing your potential). These men were talking directly to my soul, I may have moved a little to fast or maybe it was the wake up call I needed to get me out of my comfort zone. But I am now in a place to where I cannot take "NO" for an answer. Something has to turn around for me and until it does I am not allowing myself to have any days off from being the provider that my family requires of me.

Nonetheless, I realized I did move a little fast and returned back to my previous employer but for a different position purposely so that I can have some money coming in steady but enough time to focus on building myself as an entrepreneur. I have some momentum built but I am in need of more and in this continual pursuit of being the provider. I believe that being in pursuit and choosing to go on this journey, sacrificing myself makes me a provider. My season is going to change just as long as I keep moving staying focused not settling on beating the same drum and expecting different results.

When my pursuit for more on this journey brings me success, then I believe it will solidify me as a father in my home.

Supplier, donor, giver, contributor, source, breadwinner,

wage earner – Provider /prəˈvīdər/

HELP FIT

And the Lord God said, It is not good that the man should be alone; I will make him an help meet (A help fit) for him. – Genesis 2:18

What is my Help Meet? Who is my Help Fit?

Lets start by saying there is somebody for everybody, well at least that is what I believe. Here in this verse, it defines how woman was made for man and the man was made for woman. Even though they may be different they fit together like two puzzle pieces with opposite shapes but when connected they fit perfectly together.

This may seem like I'm off in center field a little but in my commitment as a father I have been noticing that I am more effective with parenting when the communication, love levels, and respect for my wife are on good terms. In other words, I believe that my children will respond to me better as a father when my relationship with their mother is healthy. So my desire then is to be a great father to my children and an excellent husband to my wife.

Furthermore, if being in a healthy relationship with my wife provided for me stable ground as a father then the preparation I made before being a father was pivotal.

I understand that every man does not have my same story of how God kept me, how God gave me the strength to abstain from promiscuity even at a young age but my process propelled me toward my promise of a great future. I am currently nine years married (2017) and every test and trial that you think would come, did come, and hitting hard. The things that we at one time found to be an easy transition has changed especially now with just two kids nothing that sustained us prior is good enough now. We need a bigger home, a bigger vehicle and I need a better job, etc. More, more, more, and bigger, bigger, bigger is all I hear in the midst of not being able to supply it properly for my family. Mind you this is just with two kids, where some people are raising five to nine children and here I am not having enough with two, so you understand how our finances are not where we need it. Then through all stress and headache of not being enough, am I required to be a great husband because it provides for me stable ground to be a good father?

In my pursuit to being a good father I have been taking more notice of how my relationship with my children's mother has given me leeway to be a good father. My children does not comprehend that their mom is my wife, my girl friend, or my one nightstand. They only know that she is mom and I am trying to be dad. I only say trying to be dad because of the phrase, "Children are born knowing mom but they have to be introduced to dad". I do not take this opportunity lightly, but I rest some of my position of being a good dad on being a great husband. I never wanted to deal with the drama of having kids out of wedlock and not just due to what I believe as an ordained minister and elder in my church. But this was a personal and spiritual opportunity toward being a good dad by first learning to be a great husband. Keeping this principle is pushing me as the man of my house to never give up on my wife. Which dismisses the notion where one would say they love their kids but cannot stand their mother. Now I could not tell you how many people have pushed their success as a dad while not having a relationship with the mother of their children but I am experimenting on utilizing the leverage I have with the love from my kids to push me to being a great husband and if successful at being a great husband would mean that I have progressed at being a good dad.

I have been with my wife for a long time, knowing her for over twenty-five years, dated her for five years, and married to her for 9 years (2017). Wow! Let's just say I am committed to one woman. After all this time though, I am pressed to produce more because of having children. Here is the key for men, I can either demand her to accept the life of hard knocks and fight day though the night until she can see it my way, that this is all I can produce. On the other hand, I can use her desire for more and dreams of better to push me toward producing better. When God made woman as a help fit, it means that they have the ability to fit or adjust to life's hardships. Women fit in positions that help men produce as well, so I say choose to allow the dreams and aspirations of your wife or mother to your children to push you to the best version of yourself.

If you have children with a woman but you have not committed yourself with marriage, I dare you to take a closer look at the mother of your children and take a deep look into her dreams for a better tomorrow then allow those dreams to connect with your hearts pulse. Yes, you would have to get emotionally involved but I am telling you it is worth it because this spiritual connection has developed me as a man taking on one of the greatest challenges in this life, the challenge of conquering the emotions of a woman.

    This has allowed me to look past my fears and put a ring on her finger as well, which is to say that I can climb any mountain and push through any valley. Just when you think you were the greatest love machine known to man, when you can conquer and commit to one woman then allow her to see that she has the gift to produce a great husband in you... When you make love to your wife it is on another level of intensity! Let me explain to you how I climbed this mountain. Before I started my journey of fatherhood I felt I needed to learn how to be "The Man" for one woman. Not being scared of commitment is what I am referring to, this is to say that before making such a commitment I was indeed terrified but from the love that I felt I was confident in my decision. This is the reason why pushed past my fear. My journey with my wife was extensive but well worth it. I first have to admit that I was blinded by love. I'll explain. Ms. Eboné (Ebony) Flowers is her name and dancing for the

Lord was her passion and I mean she is good. Growing up in the church, my wife was known as the life of the party, bubbly, the nobody can stop me – spirited dancer. Everyone enjoyed watching Eboné dance with the praise dancers or IGP as they called themselves (Instruments of God's Praise).

I wish I could tell you something interesting like I was checking her out hoping that one day she would be my wife but I can't because thoughts like that would have got me arrested. What am I talking about…? I am seven years older then my wife, so while I am a seventeen years old senior about to graduate High School my wife was ten years old. Jail, Jail, Jail! No we didn't consider ourselves to ever be in a relationship let alone marriage, we had a committed brother and sister relationship. While she grew up in the church, I started going to the church at thirteen years old and she was my little sister. I just always admired her spirit and excitement in life, she always carried herself like a young lady and I always believed that she would one day make some man happy. Then of course I was still left alone getting ready to go into college, never had a girl friend, never even came close to having female associates, I was just alone. But all of that was about to change because I didn't see myself as being alone for the rest of my life so I committed myself "**to**" prayer, well actually "**a**" prayer which consisted of all my specific details for the wife of my dreams.

Two years into college, I must say I believe I went a little bit over board but I had a lot of time to myself for being so alone I added some uncommon details to my prayer. In my prayer opportunity to talk with God about this subject, it was a little weird but being that this could be a life changing moment in my life whether positive or negative, still life changing. I asked God to bless me with a wife, but not just any wife but a woman that I am attracted too and would love to be around everyday. I considered myself to be a boring guy being such a quiet person so my next prayer was that of needing to add a little excitement in my life. Lord I need my wife to have some excitement in her life, where it may help me break out of my shell. If I considered someone that was as quiet as me, I would get too bored. Getting bored with each other is a recipe for disaster. I prayed that I would be attracted to a black woman, not wanting to bring any offense or disrespect to any other nationalities. I just figured that I was light skinned and mixing with another light skin we might create some transparent babies. I just needed a little chocolate in my life. Did I stop there, not at all I was just getting started. I was also mesmerized by big backsides (big butts if you will) and wanted my wife to be blessed in that area. Oh yeah and nice legs too, I didn't want a nice backside on my wife and little legs. Some of the things I was hoping to not have were big feet; I am in love with feet. I can't say that I have a fetish with feet but I love small well-kept feet.

Would you call this shallow, would you call this ridiculous, would you even call this ignorant? Well at the time I didn't because I was single for a long time and did not think it to be a problem to at least talk to God about a possible dream come true. I prayed about the shape of her eyes, I prayed about the pucker of her lips, I prayed about her being educated but not too sophisticated where she would give up on a guy like me. Someone that was willing to grow with me, someone that would never give up on the challenges that life would bring. As far as culture, I always loved the Spanish culture and the Caribbean culture, so if I found someone in either of these cultures I was committing all the way. Interesting enough I only dated three times in my life, well tried to date anyway. First of which was a Puerto Rican Chica, a young lady who's family was heavy into church but too strict where it pushed me out of the way because I did not fit the profile her family expected for their daughter. We actually liked each other but the only strange thing was our communication was great by text message but barely two sentences in person. I started out noticing her in one of my art classes and with the position of being a professional novice at dating I was praying even for this area of just talking to a girl with an interest in her for the first time in my life. I asked God for confirmation, which is when you pretty much ask God for proof that He is on your side. But I took it to the extreme yet again when I built up the courage to finally talk to this girl I prayed like this; "Lord, if it's ok for me to talk to this girl allow this to happen for me. When I go back to class the next day cause me to wake up late and not waking up then going back to sleep but me going to bed early until the first time I open my eyes that I am late for class". Then, when I get to school let the class be packed and only two chairs be left in the middle of the class, one for me and one for her, meaning she would have to be late as well. After I take my seat let the next person that darkens that door way to be her". You can call me crazy, you can say I went over the top but would you believe that it happened exactly as I asked. This was not a prayer for a wife but just trusting that God would guide me through the dating process. Even though it did not work out between us and did not even come close to a relationship I at least understood that on this journey toward fatherhood I had some divine help on my side. In my next semester I ran into another whom I thought could be in my life and she was Jamaican. This young lady I met in the Christian club held on the college campus and after a few months of coming to the Christian club I wanted to see if this would be a potential match for me.

I really cannot remember how that connection started up but she was still in love with her ex-boyfriend, so I never had a chance. This was my motto, to be true to yourself where if you feel reasonable doubt about a potential relationship, do not be afraid to address the issue. If something does not fit in your life, question yourself if it is really worth forcing it to work. This is because you only have one life and every moment wasted in your life you will never get back.

If something is not intended to fit in your life, why hesitate to remove it? Why get so attached where you emotionally find it difficult to let it go? I reacted immediately and let that connection go and just kept living life focusing on school. In 2003, I began getting ready to graduate college when my sister from the church asked me if I would accompany her to the prom because her date dropped out about one or two weeks before the event and she did not want to go alone. So she asked me to go, subsequently it was beneficial to me because I did not go to my prom in High School... I did not want to go alone.

College man going to a high school prom to fulfill a favor for who was considered to be a little sister in my church, this was a priceless event for me. She had the time of her life to say the least but after her prom I was back to my commitments to my church and commitment to my journey.

A new development came into my life in ministry when I began to work with the youth department and guess who was selected to work with me, my prom date. My wife will tell you I am wrong but I am telling you I am right, while we were supposed to be putting together the events for the youth she had a pressing question that she had to get answered. Does age matter to me? Mind you, all of my "little sisters" in the church were very protective of me in regards to any female that flaunted in my face. So when Eboné asked this question, which I considered it to be directed toward the general sense. How does age fit in my description for the girl I wanted to be with? I answered her; "Age isn't just a number to me only because I never saw myself with someone older than me but if she was, maybe by a few years older and the same goes for younger, only by a few years". Then she said after a long pause, "What about my age (18)?"

Now I didn't take this as her asking me out and being aggressively forward because I could say that I would date someone her age of eighteen but it didn't have to be her. This was answering the questioning about dating someone her age. Oh and my answer was I don't know. But after that phone call I will admit I looked at her differently, mainly because we still had to connect often to discuss youth ministry decisions. After every phone call we continued to talk, which led to more and more talking. This connection turned into courtship for five years and not because of anything specific why we waited so long but we were so concentrated on the joy of being together. I was not ready at that time to be a father but before I would, it was my journey to try and be good at being a husband to the future mother of my children. I understand that everybody has different life circumstances but at this stage of my life I was blessed to not have children out of wedlock and I have not been in/ out of multiple relationships. Yes, I say blessed because to me it was only by the grace of God that I was sustained in abstinence and not of my own will.

    I asked myself a question after being great friends with the same woman for five years... Can I have this for the rest of my life? If I committed to her would it work? Was I willing to take a chance at being the father to her children? Well again, I asked the Lord to confirm it for me and lets just say for the record that this is something I needed to do. In my prayer, I asked for Eboné to get her menstrual cycle late and that is because her cycle just changed and came early one month prior to this request. I understood that a woman's menstrual cycle changes periodically but not month to month.

Then to make it more interesting, just in case her cycle was abnormal and I did not know it, how about I prayed that it would come on a Wednesday. Was that enough? Not at all, lastly I prayed that she would tell me it came late without me asking but would initiate the conversation. Then if it did not pan out this way in exact detail I had to let the relationship go. This would mean that this was not my wife and I should not waste any more of her life. This may not be a plan for most men or probably not for any man if I would be honest because I am not really sure how many would go to this extreme to make sure that they would benefit the life of a woman and be a potentially good father to her children. This is my story though; this is how my journey to fatherhood started and at this stage it has been working for me. After enjoying marriage and managing the ups and downs that life would bring, once I was officially a father I pondered on an interesting test in fatherhood. The test of what is called, **"Baby Momma Drama"**– Please forgive the slang of this term but I really did not know how to continue this subject without defining this issue as it relates to being a father.

Wikipedia defines this as *being originated in Jamaican Creole as "baby-mother" (pronounced ['bebi 'mada]), with the first printed usage appearing in the Kingston newspaper, The Daily Gleaner in 1966.*

Another Daily Gleaner use dates from November 21, 1989. Originally, the term was used by the fathers of illegitimate children to describe the mothers of their children but the term is now in general use to describe any single mother. (https://en.wikipedia.org/wiki/Baby_mama)

    I want to redefine and place "Baby Momma Drama" as an issue even in the house among married people. Not having anything to do with an illegitimate situation but this issue is being the current parents of the children in the house. This is to understand that just because your married does not mean you connect on the same wavelength when parenting. When you have a father not having the same understanding on how to manage the children in the house as the mother, that misunderstanding will bring that father a heavy load of "Baby Momma Drama". Married life today is a bit misconstrued because some married couples have been together for years in the same house but sleep in separate bedrooms.

Some married people have nothing to do with each other except that they built a fortune and together they provide more money verses getting a divorce, so they stay married for the money but live single lives. When a marriage is constructed like this from the father's point of view and if at any time he stands at odds in regards to the parental views verses the mothers view, due to the lack of marital commitment he could incur some baby momma drama. This does not by any means put negativity on the mother of the children but please focus on the fact that this is an effort for the man to succeed as a father and that the father has to understand this succession will come when he provides clear, consistent, committed communication with the mother of the children. What I am focusing on here is, adding success as a father by keeping quality communication with the mother of the children. I am aware that some men have children by different women which brings me to this next point of keeping this much needed communication with the one that is mothering your children and in regards to the birth mother of the children there is always room to just show respect. Well what if the birth mother has some issues that causes you to lose your sanity? As the old adage goes, "After you make the bed, you have to lay in it", which explains what allows your children to see you as their superhero.

With all of what you deal with and struggle through, you are willing to fight through it to keep your relationship as a father to them. This is giving your life for your children which will prove you to be a better husband if you play your cards right. It has always been a pet peeve of my wife when she wasn't sure if I spent the time needed with my children, taking the time to say I love them, paying attention to questions, or learning their cries.

I could not begin to tell you the stories of grown men that are still hurting from the lack of a father in their lives. Lets be honest, not having your father in your life has nothing to do with being successful or getting ahead in life but it is another level of pain that a child has when dad doesn't stay with who they call mom. I did not want that to be my story, even with the uncertainties of what life brings, I still wanted to excel at being a great father and an outstanding husband to my wife. By focusing on such matters I believe you can avoid baby momma drama in your home when parenting your children.

When you produce what you need as a father the end result should be that you both would come to an agreement. Even if it is that you agree to your disagreement, there has to be some type of understanding.

For example, I have my own methodology to how I discipline children especially my own children, my wife however is not as strict when it comes to discipline. If they cry at a certain octave, if they keep whining over and over again or if they are not behaving, her main concern isn't discipline – at that point it is peace and quiet. On the other hand, if it is not repetitive, understood and demonstrated by following household instructions I am not satisfied. With everything there has to be balance or equilibrium so my wife came up with a phrase to use in moments like this, "Pick your battle". I am not sure where we heard this, it is a familiar phrase non-the-less.

As I fore-stated my son is a bit hyper, we deal with it and manage it as needed and this phrase allows my mind to know when to deal with it, timing is everything. You have to know the right time when to manage your children's varied behaviors. Every situation does not warrant you to deal with your children the same way when disciplining your children. Understanding this as a man will help me avoid "Baby Momma Drama". Furthermore, with this level of disciplined, comprehension there should not be arguments in front of the children, disagreements, or fussing. Communication on this level will be as a husband and wife and not as baby momma drama.

Everything that pertains to our children must result in agreement and I as the father have to learn how to communicate with my wife. Anything as relates to the developmental staging of our children I have to be able to communicate to the level of when we have to come to an agreement and avoid a civil war in my house. One thing that assists me in this process as I mentioned in the *"Discipline Chapter"* is that there is no cursing in my home, no cursing at each other. There is no excuse for any F*** words to come out of my mouth or calling my wife out of her name, no matter how frustrating things become. I, of course, give honor to God for such a grace to abstain from this type of behavior in my home. Whether you believe it or not prayer can change things and in some cases prayer changes people and people change things.

Steve Harvey has even impacted my life as he has changed the world when teaching women how to "Act Like A Lady and Think Like A Man". This was aimed to arm women on how to understand men and to shine light on so many misunderstood issues. Well, this has made it so clear to me that I need to take such an opportunity to understand my wife as well, which will provide the balance needed in my home. Women are constantly evolving due to so many pressures in life, which makes them a very self-efficient parent, so to speak.

I have to get my head out of the clouds and start growing as well in order to produce in my role as the father. I have also developed balance learning when to listen to my wife, this removes me from the phrase, "whatever she says goes". I have my way of doing a lot of things and my wife can have a different approach on how it should be handled which can be related to the children, cleaning, finances, and etcetera. Even with my opinion with how I would handle things if the suggestion of my wife sounds like it could possibly be better then I go with it.

I have my set way of doing things with my small case of OCD but I have to recant my way of thinking to work with her suggestions sometimes which turns out great and in turn creating the balance needed in my home. Sometimes my wife will call out, "Babe... Pick your battles", this is when my son is having a fit because he did not close a door or does not get something that his sister was able to get.

Sometimes it is appropriate to choose to leave the situation alone and just let him pull himself together. Other times when she would say, "Pick your battles" I would respond, "I have picked the battle and he needs a little help, with my tools of discipline. This is what I meant when I said that I have learned when to listen to my wife.

In regards to picking my battles while **fathering** my children, it kept me away from **Pharaoh-ing** over my children. We have heard that communication is the key in relationships, well how about when you utilize that key often in your relationship it also helps you become a better parent. Understand that this is whether you are with your children's mother or not, clear communication still remains to be the key to a healthy relationship. My children pay attention to how my wife and I communicate, they have open ears when we have disagreements and they focus on the times that I am affectionate towards their mother. This is why you don't just throw money at them for their birthdays, you don't break promises but you spend time, money and energy.

What you do for their mother or how you treat the one mothering them is crucial on the development of being a father.

There is a scripture I am reminded of in Ephesians 5th Chapter and the 25th verse that states: *Husbands, love your wives, just as Christ loved the church and gave himself up for her.*

You are supposed to give your life for your wife, which benefits the family. This is not an easy thing to do when considering all of the challenges that was presented just by having a second child.

We are always tired and our communication levels have been off, we haven't been dating (doing the small things to keep each other happy).

Honestly we haven't been dating since our second child, we have been playing catch up. But what I still believe is, if I, as the man, remain consistent with staying in the fight for the happiness of my wife, staying true to the marital commitment of being a husband to the mother of my children I will keep the communication levels open. Thus, I will avoid "Baby Momma Drama" and strengthen the healthy connection with my Help Fit causing me to excel as a father to my children.

THE VOW

Things in life continually change, some positive and some negative but rest a sure they will change. My stress levels are what changed for me. I typically keep a cool head in the midst of pressure but between getting to my mid-thirty's and experiencing life's challenges, I have been getting a little stressed out. My biggest stressor is finance and some would say that it is for everyone but for someone who really does not stress this came as a bombshell. Mainly because it stresses my wife out that it has become so hard to make ends to meet. With all that she does as a teacher making more than me, it has been hard to pull up my end. Have I been sitting and playing video games? NO! I have actually been posting résumés, going on interviews, trying to push my own business in graphic design, at one point I was working for a funeral home, and of course I have been writing books. I am in the push to expand one of the gifts that God has given me but nothing has come out yet even though I am hopeful. Even though these efforts are great for me as a man to never give up, I still have not produced enough finances for my family the way it is needed. This is what has brought on my greatest stressor of not being able to provide more for my children and my wife.

I feel sometimes like I fall short of being a good father, even with the backing of my wife and her never give up approach. I just want to understand how will it pull through for me as a good father. These are some of the questions that run through my head when I hold my children or prepare to put them in the bed. Even though I have these financial struggles I do not allow my kids to see me cry, I can find plenty of ways to keep smiles on their faces. When my children see me after a long day, yes they run to me. With all of my tools of discipline and training, I always find time to love on them and keep them happy and I find time to love on my wife their mom to keep her happy. Eboné has been my greatest support system even when things get stressful she still finds a way to ensure me that I am her man. This pushed me toward my consistency at being a great husband and father to my children.

Even though the lack of finances still gets to me and places small pockets of doubt in my mind, I count my blessings and thank God. Blessings such as, I do not have to deal with infidelity in my marriage and I thank God I do not have to deal with dyfs or domestic issues.

My kids are currently at the ages of four and two years old, what am I supposed to do with the many years ahead of me?

I have my faith in God that some way or some how things are going to turn around and limit the distractions from my journey into fatherhood. Truthfully, I have never lost my love for being a dad and remembering the times I stared into the faces of my children for the first time thinking about the popular poem;

"Ten fingers, Ten little toes, two little eyes and a cute little nose". I can remember being in the hospital while my wife slept, immersing myself into the eyes of this new creation and blessing. Making sure that their finger nails where all there and over looking each eyebrow. The little facial expressions made while they slept and noticing birth marks that where actually similar to mine. I had to recalculate my emotions and realize that time with my children is more important than money. I had to stop and thank God that regardless of all the struggles, my family eats everyday. This is why I spend a lot of time with my kids. This is why with all of what my wife and I have been through the fact that we made it through our struggles together is worth more than money. Our love has been tested and tried. But our personal struggles pale into comparison when trying to be a good parent.

When you want your children to excel and succeed further than you have in life, when this became my primary focus it was a bit overwhelming because I could not see how I measured up as a parent. So with all of what comes from life's uncertainties I still had to find the grace to gain my niche in this life that will bring success. I have to hold onto my faith to believe that I will gain the wisdom to excel as a father.

This was me 2:00 am in the morning trying to let my recovering wife sleep while I manage the kids. I was doing as much as I could to make sure she did not have to get up for almost anything. I had to make sure that she would not open any surgical stitches she had from her second C-Section with our second child.

    With all of this being laid on me all at once my heart and mind were battling with my faith that there has to be a better way for me. Am I going to make it as a good father to these children and be a good husband to my wife? I am not talking about tips and tricks on a daily basis to help me with parenting but I needed something that could consistently keep my mind at a state of rest that I might gain the wisdom to see a better way.

If I lose my mind - then I will lose my kids and then ultimately I will lose my family, but if I keep my mind then I maintain my place as the father in my home. It is vitally important that I maintain my place as THE FATHER in my home.

This process did not even come as a difficulty; it was a simple transition to understand but a journey to learn.

I was holding my children this one night when my daughter was a newborn crying for milk every two hours and my son was a two year old still thinking he is an only child demanding attention. Even when I developed some type of a system when needing to give bottles or change pampers, as they grew, my system kept changing. I was at my wits end on how would I keep up, as I have already explained my mindset through my journey toward fatherhood it has brought me here in front of my crossroad needing to make a clear decision of how will I make it as a father. Then as I held my kids in my arms, trying to put them to sleep I was reminded of another commitment that I made and do not intend on breaking, which was coming from the glare of the street light on my wedding ring.

I was reminded of my wedding vow that I made to my wife and how I have taken that commitment so serious. Would it be possible to make such a commitment to my children? Of course it is but I pondered on the plagiarized usage of committing to your children because you're their parents. This has not worked for so many once life struggles came in the middle. It seems like financial struggles, marital disagreements, divorce all tend to be empowered through selfishness not considering how It will affect the children. I did not want that to be my life's story so I consider empowering my commitment to my children to another level.

What if I married my children?

Now I don't mean having a ceremony with a reception and settling the guest list. No, this would not be for the lights, cameras or action but this was just between my children and me. My commitment as their father, I would make a special vow to my children and not just any vow. Did you ever consider the verbiage of the marital vows and how it can also apply to your children as their father?

It is 3:00am now and I am standing in the middle of my son's room holding both of my children with my wife sleeping peacefully in our bedroom.

I repeated these words:

I, Martin Steward, take you, Jaxon and Violette Steward, to be my children, to have and to hold, from this day forward, for better, for worse, for richer, for poorer, in sickness and in health, until death do us part according to God's holy law, this is my solemn vow.

I vow to teach you after God's ordinance in the holy estate of fatherhood. I will love you, comfort you, honor, and keep you, in sickness and in health; and, forsaking all others, keeping God first in your lives, so long as I live. So help me God.

Then I even applied this scripture, which I am not sure if it's out of context but I used it:

Mark 10:9 "Therefore what God has joined together, let no one separate."

I am vowing to not let anything that life throws my way, the stress of surviving, or the negativity of ignorant people separate me from my children.

Even more, my family.

    I AM MARRIED TO FATHERHOOD!

ABOUT THE AUTHOR

Martin Steward was born and raised in Jersey City, NJ to Georgella Steward and the late Frederick A. Steward. Martin grew up with three brothers and one sister: Curtis, Fred, Michael, and Nina. At the young age of thirteen Martin accepted Jesus Christ as his Lord and Savior. He was blessed to be able to gain accomplishments in his life. In 2003, he graduated from New Jersey City University with a B.A. in Graphic Design & Illustration. Martin Steward was also blessed to have Eboné Steward as his wife on August 2, 2008. From this union they celebrate the life of their son Jaxon Martin Steward, born July 12, 2013 and in February of 2015 they celebrate the life of their daughter Violette Ebonae

Steward, the new addition to family. Together they continue working with the youth ministry at TET Better Life Ministry, under the leadership and mentoring of Pastor Jevah L. Richardson.

As an entrepreneur, Martin Steward is a graphic designer and teacher of graphic design producing and helping people produce professional logo designs, business cards, flyers, banners, etc. As a playwright, Martin has assisted the youth department at TET Better Life Ministry to put together plays for the community. In majority of the plays Martin had an active role in the play as either a lead character or a supporting character. These plays dealt with issues such as; gang violence, rape, domestic violence, etc.

Now Martin is looking to advance his gift of writing to the world of book writing and hopefully soon Martin will look into screenwriting for movies. Martin's newest venture started with his newest literary work, "Married to Fatherhood". This book gives all and tells all about the triumphs and struggles he endured as a father. Everybody has a story to tell concerning his or her life but it takes another level of courage to write about it for the world to know. His hopes rest on the opportunity to be a blessing to someone through his story. Martin's motto while writing this book is, *"If your life has not impacted someone else while you're alive...*

Once your time here is done and you pass away, it will be as if you have never existed" –Martin Steward.

Change someone's life... Tell your story!

In 2019, Martin Steward has impacted the world again with his newest journey in writing with "The Adventures of Boogie and Tiny". This children's book comes from the mind of Jaxon Steward. As such a lively child and very opinionated it seemed obvious to find a way create something from this. Hence, we now have a string of children's books from his sons mind.

Confident of this very thing, that he which has begun a good work in you will perform it until the day of Jesus Christ: - Philippians 1:6-

Made in the USA
Middletown, DE
29 March 2019